Daily Gratitude Journal

This journal belongs to:

....

PowerofGratitude

Welcome to the Journal of Gratitude, your path to a better vision of life!

Most people know it's good to be grateful, but many don't understand what gratitude really does for us.

Expressing gratitude instantly shifts your energy. It puts you in harmony with your source of supply so that the good in everything moves toward you.

We will access a place with more joy, peace, and happiness. When you reflect on the questions in this journal, even if it lasts a few minutes a day, it is enough to bring gratitude and all its benefits in your heart, in your life, in your Universe.

I like the way Wallace Wattles puts it in "The Science of Getting Rich." He said, "The grateful mind is constantly fixed upon the best. Therefore, it tends to become the best; it takes the form or character of the best and will receive the best."

Gratitude for all aspects of your life

Day 1: Daily gratitude
Day 2: Gratitude to our ancestors
Day 3: Gratitude for the energy of our ancestors
Day 4: Gratitude to the mother
Day 5: Gratitude to my father
Day 6: Harmonious relations
Day 7: The perfect body
Day 8: The magic of the senses
Day 9: The health of my organs
Day 10: Cash flow
Day 11: The magic of money
Day 12: Resolving a negative situation
Day 13: Gratitude for the food you eat
Day 14: Gratitude for the activity you carry out
Day 15: You attract money like a magnet
Day 16: The magic of gratitude
Day 17: Magic morning
Day 18: People who have supported you throughout your life
Day 19: Create a magical day
Day 20: Wishes fulfilled
Day 21: Magic panel of wishes
Day 22: Healing relationships
Day 23: Open to receive
Day 24: Magic to-do list
Day 25: Steps of gratitude
Day 26: Gratitude from the heart
Day 27: Magical wishes
Day 28: Wonderful results
Day 29: Magic invoices
Day 30: Magic breathing
Day 31: Give thanks
Day 32: Magic signs
Day 33: Bless the mistakes
Day 34: Your perfect image
Day 35: The energy of your home
Day 36: Magic holidays
Day 37: The perfect food
Day 38: Colleagues of magic
Day 39: Gratitude for nature/environment
Day 40: Gratitude for yourself

The 40-Day Power of Gratitude Program

This program is specially designed for you to learn how to practice gratitude naturally so you can be healthier, attract more money, have harmonious relationships, get a job, or start/run a successful business, as well as fulfill your most daring desires. You will also learn how to transform negative situations or experiences.

The first step is to make a list of all the intentions you want to manifest in all areas of your life. Think in as much detail as you can about everything you want to become, have, and do in terms of your relationships, your career, your health, your finances, and in any area of your life that you want to improve.

You can organize the list of intentions by grouping them into categories: health and body, career and work, money, family relationships, friends, personal desires, material things.

Once you have clarified your intentions, the power of gratitude can operate much more efficiently in the direction you want to change your life, which means that you will attract what you want much more easily.

The Pyramid of Human Consciousness by Dr. David R. Hawkins shows us that gratitude has one of the highest vibrations, so by practicing for 40 days, you will create new neural networks and you will be able to live the life you dream of.

The more gratitude you feel for your current life, the more gratitude you will receive.
If you complain and you are dissatisfied, you will receive several reasons for dissatisfaction; it is a principle of the law of attraction.

The magic in your life is directly proportional to the gratitude you have for what you have today.

Here are 3 simple steps to understanding the power of gratitude:

1. Think and use the words "Thank you" as often as possible.
2. The more you think and say the words "Thank you," the more grateful you will feel.
3. When you think and feel more grateful, you will receive more than you asked for.

Gratitude is a feeling. The intention of the 40-Day Power of Gratitude program is that by practicing gratitude daily, you become one with this wonderful feeling because gratitude is the force that accelerates magic in your life. The deeper and more sincere the feeling of gratitude, the more your life will change positively. If you practice gratitude constantly, daily, your life will change miraculously, like you never imagined.

Next, we will show you what you will do daily in this program. Morning and evening practice must be repeated every day, so you will start and end the day in a state of gratitude.

Day 1: Daily gratitude

In the morning, preferably on waking, make a list of at least 7 things that you currently enjoy in your life, whether it is health, career, money, family, relationships, material goods, successes, opportunities, teachings, people, etc. Write for each thing on your list the reason you are grateful.

Then reread the list in your mind or out loud and for each thing thank 3 times and feel gratitude in your body as much as you can. This exercise is repeated every morning throughout the 40 days of the program.

In the evening, before going to bed, think about at least 5 things that happened during the day for which you are grateful, then write in your diary and be thankful for each of them. Repeat this practice during all 40 days of the program.

Day 2: Gratitude to our ancestors

In the morning, preferably on waking, make a list of at least 7 things that you currently enjoy in your life, whether it is health, career, money, family, relationships, material goods, successes, opportunities, teachings, people, etc. Write for each thing on your list the reason you are grateful.

Then reread the list in your mind or out loud and for each thing thank 3 times and feel gratitude in your body as much as you can.

During the day when you find free time, relax and connect with the mother of your mother and your father (ancestors support us; we have their energy in us), close your eyes, and feel GRATEFUL for the gift of life, for your life, and feel the energy of the nation that supports you.

In the evening, before going to bed, think about at least 5 things that happened during the day for which you are grateful, then write in your diary and be thankful for each of them.

Day 3: Gratitude for the energy of our ancestors

In the morning, preferably on waking, make a list of at least 7 things that you currently enjoy in your life, whether it is health, career, money, family, relationships, material goods, successes, opportunities, teachings, people, etc. Write for each thing on your list the reason you are grateful.

Then reread the list in your mind or out loud and for each thing thank 3 times and feel gratitude in your body as much as you can.

During the day when you have a few free minutes, take a few deep breaths and then say the phrase: "I allow myself to receive the energy of my mother and father. I am filled with gratitude for the gift of Life received from them." Feel the energy of the nation in your whole body for a few moments.

In the evening, before going to bed, think about at least 5 things that happened during the day for which you are grateful, then write in your diary and be thankful for each of them.

Day 4: Gratitude to the mother

In the morning, preferably on waking, make a list of at least 7 things that you currently enjoy in your life, whether it is health, career, money, family, relationships, material goods, successes, opportunities, teachings, people, etc. Write for each thing on your list the reason you are grateful.

Then reread the list in your mind or out loud and for each thing thank 3 times and feel gratitude in your body as much as you can.

Today we will practice GRATEFULNESS for your mother, the person who gave you life, and you will say: "You are my mother and I am grateful to you for giving me life. You are the best mother to me and I am the best daughter/son to you."

In the evening, before going to bed, think about at least 5 things that happened during the day for which you are grateful, then write in your diary and be thankful for each of them.

Day 5: Gratitude to my father

In the morning, preferably on waking, make a list of at least 7 things that you currently enjoy in your life, whether it is health, career, money, family, relationships, material goods, successes, opportunities, teachings, people, etc. Write for each thing on your list the reason you are grateful.

Then reread the list in your mind or out loud and for each thing thank 3 times and feel gratitude in your body as much as you can.

Today we will practice GRATEFULNESS to your father, the person who gave your life, and you will say: "You are my father and I am grateful to you for giving me life. You are the best father to me and I am the best daughter/son to you."

In the evening, before going to bed, think about at least 5 things that happened during the day for which you are grateful, then write in your diary and be thankful for each of them.

Day 6: Harmonious relations

In the morning, preferably on waking, make a list of at least 7 things that you currently enjoy in your life, whether it is health, career, money, family, relationships, material goods, successes, opportunities, teachings, people, etc. Write for each thing on your list the reason you are grateful.

Then reread the list in your mind or out loud and for each thing thank 3 times and feel gratitude in your body as much as you can.

Today you will make a technique that helps you to have harmonious relationships with all people. With each new reason of gratitude to your loved ones, your relationships will become closer and will give you more fulfillment and joy than you ever thought. First, choose 3 relationships with the people closest to you, then write down 5 reasons why you feel grateful for the existence of the first person in your life. Repeat the procedure for the other two people. Start each sentence with the magic words "Thank you" then the person's name and why you feel grateful. Reread the list at least 3 times a day.

In the evening, before going to bed, think about at least 5 things that happened during the day for which you are grateful, then write in your diary and be thankful for each of them.

Day 7: The perfect body

In the morning, preferably on waking, make a list of at least 7 things that you currently enjoy in your life, whether it is health, career, money, family, relationships, material goods, successes, opportunities, teachings, people, etc. Write for each thing on your list the reason you are grateful.

Then reread the list in your mind or out loud and for each thing thank 3 times and feel gratitude in your body as much as you can.

Please read the following paragraphs. After reading each line for a certain part of the body, close your eyes and repeat the phrase in your mind, feeling deeply grateful for that body part. When you feel grateful for it, the state of gratitude will intensify naturally. The more intense it is, the faster you will see the appearance of amazing results in your body.

Think of your feet and soles, the main means of transport throughout your life. Think about all the things you do with your feet when walking, dancing, driving... The ability to walk gives you the freedom to move and enjoy life. "THANK YOU FOR MY FEET AND SOLES." SAY IT SINCERELY AND FEEL GRATEFUL FOR THIS GREAT GIFT IN EVERY CELL IN YOUR BODY.

Step two, think about your arms, hands, and fingers, and how many things you can do with them during a day. With them you eat, cook, dress, hug... You always use these parts of the body during the day, and without them, you would depend on other people, and that's why you say and feel
gratitude: "THANK YOU FOR MY ARMS, HANDS, AND FINGERS!"

In the evening, before going to bed, think about at least 5 things that happened during the day for which you are grateful, then write in your diary and be thankful for each of them.

Day 8: The magic of the senses

In the morning, preferably on waking, make a list of at least 7 things that you currently enjoy in your life, whether it is health, career, money, family, relationships, material goods, successes, opportunities, teachings, people, etc. Write for each thing on your list the reason you are grateful.

Then reread the list in your mind or out loud and for each thing thank 3 times and feel gratitude in your body as much as you can.

Think about the 5 senses and how amazing they are.

The sense of taste gives you unparalleled pleasure every time you eat something good.
That is why you say and feel gratitude for this feeling. "Thanks for my amazing sense of taste!"
The sense of smell allows you to experience the scents of flowers, perfumes, cooking, etc., so gratefully say: "Thank you for my amazing sense of smell!"

If you did not have a sense of touch you could not tell the difference between cold or warm, soft or sharp, fine or rough. This feeling allows you to shake someone's hand with friendship. That's why you say: "Thank you for my amazing sense of touch!"

Think now about the sense of sight, which allows you to see wonderful landscapes, the faces of loved ones, to read, to admire plants and nature. Say with all your heart: "Thank you for my eyes that allow me to see!"

The sense of hearing allows you to hear the voices of others, as well as your own, in order to be able to communicate harmoniously, and you can listen to your favorite music, listen to the sounds of nature, etc. That's why you say: "Thank you for my amazing sense of hearing!"

In the evening, before going to bed, think about at least 5 things that happened during the day for which you are grateful, then write in your diary and be thankful for each of them.

Day 9: The health of my organs

In the morning, preferably on waking, make a list of at least 7 things that you currently enjoy in your life, whether it is health, career, money, family, relationships, material goods, successes, opportunities, teachings, people, etc. Write for each thing on your list the reason you are grateful.

Then reread the list in your mind or out loud and for each thing thank 3 times and feel gratitude in your body as much as you can.

The functionality of the whole body would be impossible without the help of the brain, which processes millions of pieces of information per second, so you say: "Thank you for my brain and my amazing mind!"

Think now of the millions of cells that work non-stop in your body to ensure the health and functioning of all your organs. Say: "Thank you for my healthy cells!"

Your organs support your life, filtering, purifying, and regenerating your whole body.

That's why you say and feel grateful for them: "Thank you, my organs, for working so perfectly!"

Another miracle organ is your heart. The life of all the other organs depends on its activity, and the heart maintains the flow of life throughout the body. Say with love: "Thank you for my strong and healthy heart!"

In the evening, before going to bed, think about at least 5 things that happened during the day for which you are grateful, then write in your diary and be thankful for each of them.

Day 10: Cash flow

In the morning, preferably on waking, make a list of at least 7 things that you currently enjoy in your life, whether it is health, career, money, family, relationships, material goods, successes, opportunities, teachings, people, etc. Write for each thing on your list the reason you are grateful.

Then reread the list in your mind or out loud and for each thing thank 3 times and feel gratitude in your body as much as you can.

If you do not have enough money, it is good to understand that worries, envy, jealousy, disappointments, doubts, or fears about money will never help you earn more. These negative emotions stem from a feeling of lack of gratitude for the money you have. Money laundering and price criticisms are not gestures of gratitude and will not lead to resolving your financial situation. That is why you sincerely express your gratitude for the money you have in order to amplify the flow of money in your life! Say: "Thank you and I am happy because the money comes to me from different sources, more and more, continuously!"

In the evening, before going to bed, think about at least 5 things that happened during the day for which you are grateful, then write in your diary and be thankful for each of them.

Day II: The magic of money

In the morning, preferably on waking, make a list of at least 7 things that you currently enjoy in your life, whether it is health, career, money, family, relationships, material goods, successes, opportunities, teachings, people, etc.

Write for each thing on your list the reason you are grateful. Then reread the list in your mind or out loud and for each thing thank 3 times and feel gratitude in your body as much as you can.

Sit back, relax, and remember the moments and occasions when someone else paid for you, whether it was childhood or adult life. If you express your gratitude for the money you received in the past, the number will increase in the future! Whenever you remember such a situation, say with all your heart "THANK YOU!"

Write on a banknote "THANK YOU for all the money I have received in my life!" Carry this banknote in your wallet and every time you see it, remember to be thankful for all the money you have received so far. When you feel ready, spend this money, so let it circulate in the Universe and multiply for you.

In the evening, before going to bed, think about at least 5 things that happened during the day for which you are grateful, then write in your diary and be thankful for each of them.

Day 12: Resolving a negative situation

In the morning, preferably on waking, make a list of at least 7 things that you currently enjoy in your life, whether it is health, career, money, family, relationships, material goods, successes, opportunities, teachings, people, etc. Write for each thing on your list the reason you are grateful.

Then reread the list in your mind or out loud and for each thing thank 3 times and feel gratitude in your body as much as you can.

Choose an unpleasant situation in your life that you want to solve, then write in your journal 7 reasons to be grateful for that situation. There may be reasons from the past, present, or that you think will benefit you in the future. Conclude this exercise by writing the following statement: "Thank you, thank you, thank you for this perfect solution!"

In the evening, before going to bed, think about at least 5 things that happened during the day for which you are grateful, then write in your diary and be thankful for each of them.

Day 13: Gratitude for the food you eat

In the morning, preferably on waking, make a list of at least 7 things that you currently enjoy in your life, whether it is health, career, money, family, relationships, material goods, successes, opportunities, teachings, people, etc. Write for each thing on your list the reason you are grateful.

Then reread the list in your mind or out loud and for each thing thank 3 times and feel gratitude in your body as much as you can.

Today before eating or drinking, look at the food or drink and say out loud or in your mind: "Thank you for this food that gives energy to my body, and thanks you for this drink that moisturizes my body!"

In the evening, before going to bed, think about at least 5 things that happened during the day for which you are grateful, then write in your diary and be thankful for each of them.

Day 14: Gratitude for the activity you carry out

In the morning, preferably on waking, make a list of at least 7 things that you currently enjoy in your life, whether it is health, career, money, family, relationships, material goods, successes, opportunities, teachings, people, etc. Write for each thing on your list the reason you are grateful.

Then reread the list in your mind or out loud and for each thing thank 3 times and feel gratitude in your body as much as you can.

Gratitude for the work you do is directly proportional to the rewards you receive. You are the one who controls what you receive in return for your work, through the gratitude you give!

It would be good to love the activity you carry out every day, so whether it is a job or your own business, always practice your work with enthusiasm. Even if your current job is not what you dreamed of doing in this life, the only way to get to do what you dream of is to be grateful for what you are already doing.

Imagine that today you are supervised by a invisible boss who keeps track of all your thoughts and feelings related to your current job, so your mission is to discover as many things as you can that you are grateful about for the work you do.

In the evening, before going to bed, think about at least 5 things that happened during the day for which you are grateful, then write in your diary and be thankful for each of them.

Day 15: You attract money like a magnet

In the morning, preferably on waking, make a list of at least 7 things that you currently enjoy in your life, whether it is health, career, money, family, relationships, material goods, successes, opportunities, teachings, people, etc. Write for each thing on your list the reason you are grateful.

Then reread the list in your mind or out loud and for each thing thank 3 times and feel gratitude in your body as much as you can.

Do you have fun paying your bills and taxes? Do you spend money with a feeling of gratitude and love?

Remember that it is necessary to love the flow of money that leaves you as much as you love the one which comes to you. That's why you say: "Thank you for the money. I LOVE MONEY, AND MONEY LOVES ME. I attract money like a magnet!"

In the evening, before going to bed, think about at least 5 things that happened during the day for which you are grateful, then write in your diary and be thankful for each of them.

Day 16: The magic of gratitude

In the morning, preferably on waking, make a list of at least 7 things that you currently enjoy in your life, whether it is health, career, money, family, relationships, material goods, successes, opportunities, teachings, people, etc. Write for each thing on your list the reason you are grateful.

Then reread the list in your mind or out loud and for each thing thank 3 times and feel gratitude in your body as much as you can.

Gratitude is very strong energy and it is always moving in the direction in which we focus it. If you imagine that gratitude is a magic powder, whenever you express your gratitude to a certain person, the strong positive energy of gratitude influences all those on whom you express it. Today express your gratitude and sprinkle magic dust on at least 3 loved ones for the services you have benefited from. Close your eyes and imagine that you have a magic wand and send the magic dust of gratitude to each person on your list in turn and say from the heart "Thank you!"

In the evening, before going to bed, think about at least 5 things that happened during the day for which you are grateful, then write in your diary and be thankful for each of them.

Day 17: Magic morning

In the morning, preferably on waking, make a list of at least 7 things that you currently enjoy in your life, whether it is health, career, money, family, relationships, material goods, successes, opportunities, teachings, people, etc. Write for each thing on your list the reason you are grateful.

Then reread the list in your mind or out loud and for each thing thank 3 times and feel gratitude in your body as much as you can.

In the morning when we wake up, our brain is in the alpha state, and that's why as soon as you wake up, you should say the words "THANK YOU" before you do anything else. When you fill your morning with the vibration of gratitude, you will have a day full of magic. By learning to be grateful immediately after you wake up, you will enjoy a wonderful day, so as soon as you wake up and until you are ready to leave the house, say the words "THANK YOU" for everything you do and for all the objects you use.

In the evening, before going to bed, think about at least 5 things that happened during the day for which you are grateful, then write in your diary and be thankful for each of them.

Day 18: People who have supported you throughout your life

In the morning, preferably on waking, make a list of at least 7 things that you currently enjoy in your life, whether it is health, career, money, family, relationships, material goods, successes, opportunities, teachings, people, etc.

Write for each thing on your list the reason you are grateful. Then reread the list in your mind or out loud and for each thing thank 3 times and feel gratitude in your body as much as you can.

Like all of us, I believe that you have received help, support, or advice from other people throughout your life, in times when you needed it most. Maybe some people have positively changed the whole meaning of your life through encouragement or advice. You may have forgotten about these people, so here's what to do today: quietly and without being bothered, make a list of 3 people who have played a decisive role in your life. Then individually for each of them, write in your journal WHY you are grateful to them and how much they have changed the course of your life in a beneficial way.

In the evening, before going to bed, think about at least 5 things that happened during the day for which you are grateful, then write in your diary and be thankful for each of them.

Day 19: Create a magical day

In the morning, preferably on waking, make a list of at least 7 things that you currently enjoy in your life, whether it is health, career, money, family, relationships, material goods, successes, opportunities, teachings, people, etc. Write for each thing on your list the reason you are grateful.

Then reread the list in your mind or out loud and for each thing thank 3 times and feel gratitude in your body as much as you can.

During the morning, make a shortlist of the most important activities of the day and be thankful from the bottom of your heart for their impeccable development. Imagine all the plans you have written down and say the words "THANK YOU" and feel deep gratitude for everything that went so well for you.

In the evening, before going to bed, think about at least 5 things that happened during the day for which you are grateful, then write in your diary and be thankful for each of them.

Day 20: Wishes fulfilled

In the morning, preferably on waking, make a list of at least 7 things that you currently enjoy in your life, whether it is health, career, money, family, relationships, material goods, successes, opportunities, teachings, people, etc. Write for each thing on your list the reason you are grateful.

Then reread the list in your mind or out loud and for each thing thank 3 times and feel gratitude in your body as much as you can.

Choose 10 wishes (the most important) from those written at the beginning of the program and rewrite them as follows: "Thank you, thank you, thank you" before each one, then the wish at the present time.

Imagine that the wish has already been fulfilled and answer mentally the following questions:

1. What emotions did you feel when your wish was fulfilled?

2. Who was the first person you told that your wish was fulfilled and how did you express yourself?

3. What was the first thing you did when you found out that your wish had been fulfilled?

At the end, read the list of fulfilled wishes, emphasizing the magic words, "thank you," so that you feel the state of gratitude as intensely as possible!

In the evening, before going to bed, think about at least 5 things that happened during the day for which you are grateful, then write in your diary and be thankful for each of them.

Day 21: Magic panel of wishes

In the morning, preferably on waking, make a list of at least 7 things that you currently enjoy in your life, whether it is health, career, money, family, relationships, material goods, successes, opportunities, teachings, people, etc. Write for each thing on your list the reason you are grateful.

Then reread the list in your mind or out loud and for each thing thank 3 times and feel gratitude in your body as much as you can. Create a magic wish panel by pasting on it images associated with the 10 wishes you wrote in the diary yesterday. You can cut images from magazines or you can paste images found on the internet, images that make your heart sing.

Place the panel in a place where you can see it as often as possible. Looking at images is the key to attracting and keeping desires alive and energized. Stick on this panel the magic words "THANK YOU, THANK YOU, THANK YOU!"

In the evening, before going to bed, think about at least 5 things that happened during the day for which you are grateful, then write in your diary and be thankful for each of them.

Day 22: Healing relationships

In the morning, preferably on waking, make a list of at least 7 things that you currently enjoy in your life, whether it is health, career, money, family, relationships, material goods, successes, opportunities, teachings, people, etc. Write for each thing on your list the reason you are grateful.

Then reread the list in your mind or out loud and for each thing thank 3 times and feel gratitude in your body as much as you can.

Choose a difficult, problematic, or broken relationship that you want to heal.

Write a list of 10 things you feel grateful for. Adhere to the person's name and express your gratitude to him, then write in as much detail as possible why you are grateful to him.

In the evening, before going to bed, think about at least 5 things that happened during the day for which you are grateful, then write in your diary and be thankful for each of them.

Day 23: Open to receive

In the morning, preferably on waking, make a list of at least 7 things that you currently enjoy in your life, whether it is health, career, money, family, relationships, material goods, successes, opportunities, teachings, people, etc. Write for each thing on your list the reason you are grateful.

Then reread the list in your mind or out loud and for each thing thank 3 times and feel gratitude in your body as much as you can.

Draw a circle, then inside it write the amount of money you want to receive, your name, and today's date. Hold the circle between your palms and think about the thing you want to buy or do with this money.

Feel happy and grateful that you received this money. Put the drawing with the circle in a place where you can see it daily. When you receive the money or something you want, complete a new circle, and follow the steps above.

In the evening, before going to bed, think about at least 5 things that happened during the day for which you are grateful, then write in your diary and be thankful for each of them.

Day 24: Magic to-do list

In the morning, preferably on waking, make a list of at least 7 things that you currently enjoy in your life, whether it is health, career, money, family, relationships, material goods, successes, opportunities, teachings, people, etc. Write for each thing on your list the reason you are grateful.

Then reread the list in your mind or out loud and for each thing thank 3 times and feel gratitude in your body as much as you can.

Write a list of 3 important things in your life that you would like to solve as quickly and in a wonderful way and name this list "the magic list of things to do."

Take each situation one at a time and visualize for at least 1 minute for each situation that it has been miraculously resolved, fill yourself with gratitude, and then say "thank you" from the bottom of your heart.

In the evening, before going to bed, think about at least 5 things that happened during the day for which you are grateful, then write in your diary and be thankful for each of them.

Day 25: Steps of gratitude

In the morning, preferably on waking, make a list of at least 7 things that you currently enjoy in your life, whether it is health, career, money, family, relationships, material goods, successes, opportunities, teachings, people, etc. Write for each thing on your list the reason you are grateful.

Then reread the list in your mind or out loud and for each thing thank 3 times and feel gratitude in your body as much as you can.

Today we will practice gratitude with your magic steps.

All you have to do is, every time you take a step, say "Thank you." Do this as many times as you want during the day for at least 90 steps once.

In the evening, before going to bed, think about at least 5 things that happened during the day for which you are grateful, then write in your diary and be thankful for each of them.

Day 26: Gratitude from the heart

In the morning, preferably on waking, make a list of at least 7 things that you currently enjoy in your life, whether it is health, career, money, family, relationships, material goods, successes, opportunities, teachings, people, etc. Write for each thing on your list the reason you are grateful.

Then reread the list in your mind or out loud and for each thing thank 3 times and feel gratitude in your body as much as you can.

Focus on your heart (place your right hand on your chest), close your eyes, and repeat the words "Thank you" slowly!

Take your list of the 10 wishes and read aloud every wish on the list. At the end, close your eyes, pay attention to your heart, and say the words "Thank you" several times, slowly.

In the evening, before going to bed, think about at least 5 things that happened during the day for which you are grateful, then write in your diary and be thankful for each of them.

Day 27: Magical wishes

In the morning, preferably on waking, make a list of at least 7 things that you currently enjoy in your life, whether it is health, career, money, family, relationships, material goods, successes, opportunities, teachings, people, etc. Write for each thing on your list the reason you are grateful.

Then reread the list in your mind or out loud and for each thing thank 3 times and feel gratitude in your body as much as you can.

At the beginning of the day, take your list of the 10 wishes, reread each wish on the list, and imagine for a few minutes that each one has been fulfilled. Fill yourself with deep gratitude, as if you were enjoying the fulfillment of your desire right now.

Repeat this exercise 3 times during the day, read each wish, and feel as grateful as possible for fulfilling each one. In the evening, before going to bed, think about at least 5 things that happened during the day for which you are grateful, then write in your diary and be thankful for each of them.

Day 28: Wonderful results

In the morning, preferably on waking, make a list of at least 7 things that you currently enjoy in your life, whether it is health, career, money, family, relationships, material goods, successes, opportunities, teachings, people, etc. Write for each thing on your list the reason you are grateful.

Then reread the list in your mind or out loud and for each thing thank 3 times and feel gratitude in your body as much as you can.

During the morning, choose 3 situations for which you want to receive immediate results during the day, then write them down in your diary as if you have written them after they happened: Thanks for the wonderful result of...!

In the evening, before going to bed, think about at least 5 things that happened during the day for which you are grateful, then write in your diary and be thankful for each of them.

Day 29: Magic invoices

In the morning, preferably on waking, make a list of at least 7 things that you currently enjoy in your life, whether it is health, career, money, family, relationships, material goods, successes, opportunities, teachings, people, etc. Write for each thing on your list the reason you are grateful.

Then reread the list in your mind or out loud and for each thing thank 3 times and feel gratitude in your body as much as you can.

Today you collect all the unpaid bills and write on each bill "Thank you for the money!" Feel grateful that you have the money to pay the bills, whether you have it or not. Then look for some older invoices, which are paid, and write on the invoice "Thank you — Paid" and feel grateful that you had money to pay them.

In the evening, before going to bed, think about at least 5 things that happened during the day for which you are grateful, then write in your diary and be thankful for each of them.

Day 30: Magic breathing

In the morning, preferably on waking, make a list of at least 7 things that you currently enjoy in your life, whether it is health, career, money, family, relationships, material goods, successes, opportunities, teachings, people, etc. Write for each thing on your list the reason you are grateful.

Then reread the list in your mind or out loud and for each thing thank 3 times and feel gratitude in your body as much as you can.

During the day, become aware of the air you breathe. Do this exercise 3 times a day: Take a deep breath, feel the air fill your lungs and then your abdomen, then slowly exhale all the air. After each set of breaths, say, "Thank you for the air I breathe." Fill yourself with deep gratitude for the air that keeps you alive.

In the evening, before going to bed, think about at least 5 things that happened during the day for which you are grateful, then write in your diary and be thankful for each of them.

Day 31: Give thanks

In the morning, preferably on waking, make a list of at least 7 things that you currently enjoy in your life, whether it is health, career, money, family, relationships, material goods, successes, opportunities, teachings, people, etc. Write for each thing on your list the reason you are grateful.

Then reread the list in your mind or out loud and for each thing thank 3 times and feel gratitude in your body as much as you can.

Choose 3 close people you want to help with more health, prosperity, or happiness.

One by one, take a photo of each person (it can also be on the phone), close your eyes, and visualize for a minute how you receive the good news that that person has an increasingly better situation from all points of view.

Open your eyes, look at the photo, and say, "Thank you, thank you, thank you for your health, prosperity, or happiness (person's name)." Repeat steps for all the people you have chosen.

In the evening, before going to bed, think about at least 5 things that happened during the day for which you are grateful, then write in your diary and be thankful for each of them.

Day 32: Magic signs

In the morning, preferably on waking, make a list of at least 7 things that you currently enjoy in your life, whether it is health, career, money, family, relationships, material goods, successes, opportunities, teachings, people, etc. Write for each thing on your list the reason you are grateful.

Then reread the list in your mind or out loud and for each thing thank 3 times and feel gratitude in your body as much as you can.

Today it is necessary to be as present as possible and to identify the magic signs. Magic signs are messages from the Universe that remind you to be grateful for what you have.

For example, you hear an ambulance, then you remember to be grateful for your health. When you pass an ATM, you can be grateful for your money. Today it is necessary to identify at least 7 such magical signs.

In the evening, before going to bed, think about at least 5 things that happened during the day for which you are grateful, then write in your diary and be thankful for each of them.

Day 33: Bless the mistakes

In the morning, preferably on waking, make a list of at least 7 things that you currently enjoy in your life, whether it is health, career, money, family, relationships, material goods, successes, opportunities, teachings, people, etc. Write for each thing on your list the reason you are grateful.

Then reread the list in your mind or out loud and for each thing thank 3 times and feel gratitude in your body as much as you can.

Choose a situation in which you think you were wrong in your life.

Ask yourself: What did I learn from this mistake?

What are the good things that came out of this mistake? Find at least 7 things you have learned and be grateful for them.

In the evening, before going to bed, think about at least 5 things that happened during the day for which you are grateful, then write in your diary and be thankful for each of them.

Day 34: Your perfect image

In the morning, preferably on waking, make a list of at least 7 things that you currently enjoy in your life, whether it is health, career, money, family, relationships, material goods, successes, opportunities, teachings, people, etc. Write for each thing on your list the reason you are grateful.

Then reread the list in your mind or out loud and for each thing thank 3 times and feel gratitude in your body as much as you can.

Every time you look in the mirror today, say thank you for your image, with deep gratitude, and add 3 reasons why you feel grateful that you exist.

In the evening, before going to bed, think about at least 5 things that happened during the day for which you are grateful, then write in your diary and be thankful for each of them.

Day 35: The energy of your home

In the morning, preferably on waking, make a list of at least 7 things that you currently enjoy in your life, whether it is health, career, money, family, relationships, material goods, successes, opportunities, teachings, people, etc. Write for each thing on your list the reason you are grateful.

Then reread the list in your mind or out loud and for each thing thank 3 times and feel gratitude in your body as much as you can.

Today you need to find 10 things for which you are grateful for. It may seem normal to live in your house, but think about how many people do not have a place to live. It doesn't matter if it is your home or not, it is important to feel grateful for the place where you spend a large part of your life.

In the evening, before going to bed, think about at least 5 things that happened during the day for which you are grateful, then write in your diary and be thankful for each of them.

Day 36: Magic holidays

In the morning, preferably on waking, make a list of at least 7 things that you currently enjoy in your life, whether it is health, career, money, family, relationships, material goods, successes, opportunities, teachings, people, etc. Write for each thing on your list the reason you are grateful.

Then reread the list in your mind or out loud and for each thing thank 3 times and feel gratitude in your body as much as you can.

Please remember today at least 5 places you visited and were delighted, then write in your diary what you liked about these places and live the emotion of gratitude that your health and financial condition allowed you to see those lovely places.

In the evening, before going to bed, think about at least 5 things that happened during the day for which you are grateful, then write in your diary and be thankful for each of them.

Day 37: The perfect food

In the morning, preferably on waking, make a list of at least 7 things that you currently enjoy in your life, whether it is health, career, money, family, relationships, material goods, successes, opportunities, teachings, people, etc. Write for each thing on your list the reason you are grateful.

Then reread the list in your mind or out loud and for each thing thank 3 times and feel gratitude in your body as much as you can.

During today, before each meal, you have the exercise of blessing the food you are going to eat. It may seem trivial and natural to eat, but think that on this earth there are still people who have nothing to eat and nothing to give their children to eat.

If you happen to go to the restaurant while you wait for the food, imagine that the food will taste perfect, exactly as you like it the most, and say in your mind: "Thank you to the chef because he cooks my food exactly as I like it."

In the evening, before going to bed, think about at least 5 things that happened during the day for which you are grateful, then write in your diary and be thankful for each of them.

Day 38: Colleagues of magic

In the morning, preferably on waking, make a list of at least 7 things that you currently enjoy in your life, whether it is health, career, money, family, relationships, material goods, successes, opportunities, teachings, people, etc. Write for each thing on your list the reason you are grateful.

Then reread the list in your mind or out loud and for each thing thank 3 times and feel gratitude in your body as much as you can.

Today your attention will be focused on colleagues. We spend almost half the day in the company of colleagues, so we will give them a day to thank them. You may not have the same values or concepts as some of your colleagues, but it is good to understand that if you look for the positive parts and focus on them, the atmosphere and energy between you changes, so today look for at least three qualities for each colleague.

Thank them in your mind for these qualities and for the time spent together.

In the evening, before going to bed, think about at least 5 things that happened during the day for which you are grateful, then write in your diary and be thankful for each of them.

Day 39: Gratitude for nature/environment

In the morning, preferably on waking, make a list of at least 7 things that you currently enjoy in your life, whether it is health, career, money, family, relationships, material goods, successes, opportunities, teachings, people, etc. Write for each thing on your list the reason you are grateful.

Then reread the list in your mind or out loud and for each thing thank 3 times and feel gratitude in your body as much as you can.

On this day, you will express your gratitude to nature and the environment, so please find 7 reasons why you are grateful and write them down in your journal. Here are some examples: I am grateful to the earth for supporting me at every moment, thank you for the trees that clean the air, etc.

In the evening, before going to bed, think about at least 5 things that happened during the day for which you are grateful, then write in your diary and be thankful for each of them.

Day 40: Gratitude for yourself

In the morning, preferably on waking, make a list of at least 7 things that you currently enjoy in your life, whether it is health, career, money, family, relationships, material goods, successes, opportunities, teachings, people, etc. Write for each thing on your list the reason you are grateful.

Then reread the list in your mind or out loud and for each thing thank 3 times and feel gratitude in your body as much as you can.

Today, on this wonderful day, you will thank yourself. Please express your gratitude for at least 7 positive points of yours. For example:

Thank you for always having the feeling of strength or courage.

Thank you for having a big and loving heart.

Thank you for being a person who communicates effectively.

Thank you for having the ability to choose what is necessary for me and bring me joy.

You are the most important person in your life, and you are wonderful! You have gone through this program and we are convinced that it has brought major benefits in your life. If you want to continue to practice gratitude we warmly recommend you always do the technique you practiced every night with at least 5 wonderful things that happened to you during the day.

In the evening, before going to bed, think about at least 5 things that happened during the day for which you are grateful, then write in your diary and be thankful for each of them.

ALL RIGHTS RESERVED!

No part of this publication may be reproduced or transmitted in any form whatsoever, electronic, or mechanical, including photocopying recording, or by any informational storage or retrieval system without express written, dated and signed permission from the author.

Day 1:

Day 2:

Day 3:

Day 4:

Day 5:

Day 6:

Day 7:

Day 8:

Day 9:

Day 10:

Day 11:

Day 12:

Day 13:

Day 14:

Day 15:

Day 16:

Day 17:

Day 18:

Day 19:

Day 20:

Day 21:

Day 22:

Day 23:

Day 24:

Day 25:

Day 26:

Day 27:

Day 28:

Day 29:

Day 30:

Day 31:

Day 32:

Day 33:

Day 34:

Day 35:

Day 36:

Day 37:

Day 38:

Day 39:

Day 40:

Thank you

We hope you enjoyed our book.

As a small family company, your feedback is very important to us.

Please let us know how you like our book at:
powerofgratitude2020@gmail.com

 *@powerofgratitude2020*

 *@power_of_gratitude_*

© Copyright 2020 - All rights reserved.

You may not reproduce, duplicate or send the contents of this book without direct written permission from the author. You cannot hereby despite any circumstance blame the publisher or hold him or her to legal responsibility for any reparation, compensations, or monetary forfeiture owing to the information included herein, either in a direct or an indirect way.

Legal Notice: This book has copyright protection. You can use the book for personal purposes. You should not sell, use, alter, distribute, quote, take excerpts, or paraphrase in part or whole the material contained in this book without obtaining the permission of the author first.

Disclaimer Notice: You must take note that the information in this document is for casual reading and entertainment purposes only. We have made every attempt to provide accurate, up-to-date, and reliable information. We do not express or imply guarantees of any kind. The persons who read admit that the writer is not occupied in giving legal, financial, medical, or other advice. We put this book content by sourcing various places. Please consult a licensed professional before you try any techniques shown in this book. By going through this document, the book lover comes to an agreement that under no situation is the author accountable for any forfeiture, direct or indirect, which they may incur because of the use of material contained in this document, including, but not limited to, - errors, omissions, or inaccuracies.

www.ingramcontent.com/pod-product-compliance
Lightning Source LLC
LaVergne TN
LVHW011718060526
838200LV00051B/2938